But Do You Possess Your Soul?

Aaron Lawrence

Copyright © 2012 Aaron Lawrence

All rights reserved.

ISBN: 1-78280-878-7
ISBN-13: 978-1-78280-878-7

DEDICATION

Dad, thank you for always believing in me and encouraging me to believe in myself, I hope this book finds you well. Mom, thank you for developing my artistic mind. Grandma, may your soul rest in peace, thank you for all your wisdom and poetry.

CONTENTS

	Acknowledgments	i
1	The King and the Military	1
2	Wild Beasts and the Land	7
3	The Woman and God	18
4	Neo-colonialism and Belief	31
5	The Glory of Kings	33
6	Chapter Six	48

ACKNOWLEDGMENTS

Dejene Kasse, even your general conversation has been invaluable to me. Vicky Gayle, thank you for lending your eye to my work, your criticism has also been invaluable. Elizabeth Osiguwa of "LizIt Designs" thank you for your wonderful cover design work. Brother Judah, Brother Zadok and Brother Blue of the NMP in affiliation with the Congregation of Israel, as well as Brother RafaYah Uzzyah, without you I would never have even considered the ways of all that is done under heaven, I would never have considered my own impression upon society, I would never have had the line of interest and consequently the information to write this book. All praises to the divine intellect of the universe.

CHAPTER ONE: THE KING AND THE MILITARY

The King

In opening this discourse I will interpret a quote found at the beginning of the Kebra Nagast, or translated "Glory of Kings." The Kebra Nagast is a 14th century Ethiopian Orthodox compilation of writings detailing the Ethiopian perspective of their place in biblical history. Most famously it depicts how Menelik, the first son of King Solomon, born to the Ethiopian Queen of Sheba, was brought back to Ethiopia beginning the monarchical lineage His Imperial Majesty Haile Selassie is said to have descended from:

"When I was in the pit I pondered over this matter, and over the folly of the kings of

Armenia, and I said, in so far as I can conceive it, in what doth the greatness of kings consist? Is it in the multitude of soldiers, or in the splendor of worldly possessions, or in extent of rule over cities and towns? This was my thought each time of my prayer, and my thought stirred me again and again to meditate upon the greatness of kings. And now I will begin." - Kebra Nagast

When I was in lowly estate I pondered over this matter, and the source of other men's foolishness, and I asked myself, as far as I can understand, what makes an individual honorable? What is the true greatness of one's self? Is it in the power of his word, or opulence, or the reach of his influence? This was continuously the meditation of my heart, stirring me over and over to ponder what is worthy of esteem. And now I will begin:

Firstly, in the above, where the Kebra Nagast has said 'glory of kings' I have chosen to use 'greatness of one's self' because the rational mind is the government of a person just as a king is often synonymous with the government of people:

The Levites are a tribe of Israelites who, as a tribe, functioned in ancient times as the 'mind' of the Israelites (Moses was a Levite). They were the priesthood dedicated to studying and implementing the justice of YHWH, their God. There is evidence of a community of Levites who had found their way into ancient China, they had a temple called the "Pure and Truth Temple" which had been destroyed, and during the rebuilding of the temple around 1489, one thing inscribed was this (speaking of the process in which the Patriarchal sages rectified themselves):

Then "they purified their natural rulers" (mind) Then "they rectified their natural senses."

The mind was purified before the senses were rectified just as a king must set himself right before he attempts to govern his people, and so the first entity we will identify is our natural ruler, by whom our affairs are orchestrated.

The Military

Secondly, where the Kebra Nagast has used 'multitude of soldiers' I have used "power of his words" and instead of 'extent of rule over cities and towns' I have used "reach of his influence" because just as army soldiers gain rule over cities and towns, great orators gain influence with their words.

According to Philo - the Alexandrian Jewish philosopher - it is a mercy speech is withheld from beasts, as a beast with the gift of speech would be comparable to mad man wielding a sword. In my observation, speech is also withheld from a child, but unlike the beast, little by little the child is granted speech, and according to order should be growing in wisdom parallel to its speech until the dominion of reason surpasses that of a beast. However, speech is not withheld from a child even if correction has been, and this also is comparable to a mad man wielding a sword (or in our case, a wild king with command over a military).

There is no mighty difference between a spiritual war and an intellectual one, for one's spiritual well being depends upon their intellectual state, or understanding – as well as sincerity in what is understood. This is why religious proselytizers, who are no different to political campaigners, battle each other for control over the minds of potential subjects. This is the reason people who declare a truth are usually made enemies of the state or are martyred; such as the African American reformer el-Hajj Malik el-Shabazz, the Greek philosopher Socrates, the Sikh Guru Arjan, the Hebrew prophet Jesus Christ, the Brazilian communistic preacher Antonio Conselheiro and the Arab prophet Mohammed (pbuh). Speakers of truth or change are made greater enemies than those who merely harm the body because words are the military of the mind, and life beyond the flesh is only a war of minds for the government of other minds. In order to govern a king who is aware of himself, it is first necessary to break him and his kingdom, which is why the African slaves in America over time were taken from their parents and moved from plantation to plantation; so they could not be taught their heritage (even the average African American today does not know from where they came, they can only speculate), they were slowly conditioned into believing their slavery to be a product of nature, the "will of God". This is how the king is broken with his children never claiming the throne they are not aware of being estranged to: This is how we, the low wage laborers, believe our position in capitalism to be "just the way life works" without considering how we and those worse off than us have come to be and remain in this position.

Now we have established the reasoning as to why a person's mind – ability to reason - is their king and government, we can see with what affection I have written this book by reinterpreting a quote from the honorable Marcus Garvey through the same lens:

"Where is the black man's Government? Where is his king and his kingdom? Where is his President, his Country, and his ambassador, his army, his navy, his men of big affairs? I could not find them, and then I declared, I will help to make them."

Where is the working man's [and woman's] mind? Could we not be so much more than what we are? But many of us are herded through life as cattle because we are happy to remain in this respective state of consciousness. Ignorance, greed, consumerism, covetousness, materialism, and one-upmanship are just a few of the societal cancers we endure; the internal culture of moral, intellectual and economic stagnation keeping us from progression as a people. Many of us are so concerned with scripted politics from television shows to music and the virtue-less values projected by such mediums we forget the politics within ourselves, not realizing our natural ruler, our mind, has been dethroned, and thus we live as wild beasts given to a base and debased nature; a state governed by the whims of emotion and poverty.

CHAPTER TWO: WILD BEASTS AND THE LAND

The beast

One reason our conscience feels justified in eating animals is their having a lower state of consciousness as far as we can tell. Could this be why the rich who are better educated, as far as they can tell, feel justified in devouring the poor?

For those who will jump to a conclusion of me equating riches with evil I will quickly justify my point: It was not the poor who instituted slavery or colonialism, it is the rich who are fat from the labor of the poor, who directly benefit from war, who make and bend laws to suit themselves, who buy and privatize water sources in poor countries to bottle the water and sell it back to people who no longer have access to it, who created eunuchs to serve in their palaces, who capitalize on poverty by posing as charities yet pay themselves ludicrous amounts while doing the least to help the suffering, who, when driven solely by capital, pay the worker less than his worth. It is in power and for power one exploits, not in weakness or for weakness. Walter Rodney summed this up best in his 1972 book "How Europe Underdeveloped Africa":

"It is a common myth within capitalist thought that the individual through drive and hard work can become a capitalist. In the USA, it is usual to refer to an individual like John D. Rockerfeller, Sr., as someone who rose from 'rags to riches.' To complete the moral of the Rockerfeller success story, it would be necessary to fill in the details on all the millions of people who had to be exploited in order for one man to become a multimillionaire. The acquisition of wealth is not due to hard work alone, or the Africans working as slaves in America and the West Indies would have been the wealthiest group in the world. The individualism of the capitalist must be seen against the hard and unrewarded work of the masses."

Referring back to the statement 'one reason our conscience feels justified in eating animals is their having a lower state of consciousness as far as we can tell', this is not as much an apologism for veganism as it is to expose the heart; in the same way man devours living, feeling creatures on the grounds of deeming them stupid, so man does to man:

"The Aborigines were deemed to be subhuman, little more than animals, which was to justify not only the theft of their land, but their extermination." – John Pilger, Australian Journalist

"In the United States, where slavery was profitable and permitted, an American school of anthropology rose to defend its moral and ethical basis. To this end it was necessary to refute the idea that Negroes had had anything to do with the glories of ancient Egypt or with any other expression of civilization or high culture." – Tudor Parfitt, British Historian

"Therefore, the Negro nations are, as a rule, submissive to slavery, because they have little that is essentially human and have attributes that are quite similar to those of dumb animals, as we have stated" – Ibn Khaldun, 14th century

Tunisian Arab Historian

Subconsciously, by the same philosophy man uses to justify eating meat, he has also justified himself in conquering and destroying entire peoples for his own benefit.

What is supposed to set the human apart from the beasts is an uncanny ability to interpret and manipulate his reality. In keeping people in a state of being unable to interpret and ultimately manipulate their reality you render them useless to themselves, ready to be exploited and devoured as the beasts of the field; this, as in the case of the Negro and the Aboriginal, is often done through a denial and selective writing of their history as well as pacification concerning their current reality, both of which define their present condition. An issue which has affected the descendants of slaves in Europe and the Americas is the struggle for identity; we do not know who we are. Many of us seek an identity in the glories of Egypt, many of us claim the whole of Africa as if all Africa is one nationality (there are over 80 nationalities in Ethiopia alone), to this day some are ashamed to be considered African, some claim we are Hebrews and others claim we are Moors, some claim we are gods and others claim the blocks they live in. We war intellectually to establish ourselves according to a context we were forced into, just as the Africans in Nigeria and Cameroon still fight over Bakassi, a border created by Europeans! This confusion and madness has found its way into the heart of the working people; we fight to defend an identity which was given to us rather than define ourselves, we are quicker to fight for higher wages than to attempt restructuring ourselves outside the context of wage labor. It is said of Old Stone Age hunter gatherers they did not know how to cultivate land, only how to scavenge; their basic concern for immediate survival did not exceed the ape or the lion or the antelope and so they were tossed to and fro by the whims of nature just as animals are. 'Civilized man' does not know how to manufacture anything entirely but he is a scavenger in his own right; he is a consumer. The average citizen is helplessly tossed to and fro by the whims of commerce, unable to manipulate the financial environment to their benefit because they cannot interpret their environment; they merely happen to exist in it and are subject to it, just as the animals are. Old Stone Age man did not cultivate his land, modern man does not cultivate his time; both are bound to be extinct. We hunt and gather jobs in an environment designed for the minority rather than analyzing our condition in order to change it with the power of reason gifted to man. Just as the animal lives as a reactionary to its environment rather than revolutionizing it, so do the emotions react to stimuli yet rarely revolutionize the cause. It is in refusing to transcend this state of beast-like, ignorant, emotional, consciousness we become the livestock of a superior intelligence; the beast which is capitalized on, who works the field, who carries the master's burden is only fit for such dominion by way of inferior self-government and intelligence – which is why slaves were not allowed to read, and it is no coincidence the average proletariat is financially illiterate. The beast has no concept of God beyond its habitat, and the low wage laborer cannot see life beyond his next paycheck.

Land

Nature is defined by the manner in which it occupies the land and our lives are defined by the manner in which we occupy our time; therefore the land in our mental kingdom will be used to represent time. In life there is a point in which all ask themselves "who am I?", but it is much more worthwhile to ask "what is my occupation?"

Land has been heavily misused by man, and in the form of territory it has been fought over since the beginning of documented history; whether we look at how land is being forcefully or manipulatively confiscated from local farmers in Africa in order to give to Asian and Arab business-men for the mass production of single crops, or how the land of indigenous Australians was and is being stolen by European descendants in order to build their own state, mine mineral rich areas and control all profitability from the earth. Your time is also a territory sought after by those who seek to profit from it - time, the first land you can ever truly own. As is common knowledge, many blacks brought through the trans-Atlantic slave trade were sold or stolen from their land to labor for the well-being of another land; that form of slavery is over for most of us, but what land do we now call ours? Part of holding power in the Earth is primarily to own and control land, which is necessary for sustenance, manufacturing, laboring and any human activity including all things survival orientated. Like a family without a house who must beg for stay under another's roof in order to survive, it is a pitiful thing for a nation not to own land – and like a nation without land, it is a pitiful thing for a person to have no control over their own time.

To show the average person does not possess their life, let us examine this: In the UK – at least on paper - the average soul works at least 8 hours a day for someone else; let's say time spent traveling to and from work takes two hours in total, getting ready for work takes another hour, by the time they get home they must cook and eat (another hour), that's 12 hours out of the person's day where their mind is geared towards going to work or winding down from work. The recommended amount of sleep for an adult is 8 hours, 8+12=20, out of 24 hours in a day this leaves 4 hours to raise their children, engage with their spouse, run errands, study etc, which is ok as long as one has no other aspirations and is not aware that they are being robbed of the most precious resource; time. Bear in mind 8 hour days 5 days a week on minimum wage is not enough for the average single person to survive without debt in cities like London, they may be able to rent a room in a shared house but they surely can't own a car or even travel by bus regularly on this pay as rent, tax and living expenses like food will leave them as paupers waiting for the next paycheck. This brief example does not take into account those poor souls who work seven days a week doing cash-in-hand jobs in which it is not uncommon to earn £5 pounds an hour, barely enough to survive considering the cost of living in Britain – these slaves who live only to work, stuck trying to support a family or create a life from low wages are the broken backs upholding the glamour of their country - like Mayan workers in Cancun who go unseen, working tirelessly in US or European owned hotels for little pay on temporary contracts of employment to facilitate and pick up after the carnage left behind by oblivious, partying, foreign spring-breakers. People must borrow, overwork themselves, put themselves in debt or steal and cheat in order to live; many an honest worker has been swallowed up by the system, robbed by bailiffs, fined, or prosecuted for being unable to sustain even simple lives on thin wages without debt, staying barely afloat until the legal grim reaper comes-a-knocking. For people with their own plans to accomplish, what time, money, or energy do they have left to cultivate their minds, and consequently, their lives? People who have no time for themselves have no time to figure out what system they are in, let alone to define themselves within or without it, this means they have no purpose other than to produce capital for someone else, and to keep themselves alive in order to have the privilege of doing so. Time only remains to be squandered on entertainment to be eased of the mind numbing monotony called "work" consuming their days. It is good to work, but as we will see later in this book, to work solely for another king only destroys the integrity of one's own state. This piece of Hebrew philosophy found in the apocrypha sums up the importance of time: "The wisdom of a learned man cometh by opportunity of leisure; and he that hath little business shall become wise. How can he get wisdom that holdeth the plough, and that glorieth in the goad, that driveth oxen, and is occupied in their labours, and whose talk is of bullocks?" - Sirach 38:24-25

The king must recognize how valuable his land is; that is to say a person must value their time. What king has no land? Land is the most precious asset, yet we allow it to be consumed by fruitlessness and counter-productivity, we sell our land to foreigners and our time to the uncertainty of wage-labor, and squander the little time we have left on unprofitable relationships. All nature thrives off interdependency if we are to learn from it, but interdependence is only worthwhile among those who are like-minded and of one accord;

self sufficiency is power as long as a cry for a help is seen as a gap in the market and debt is the underbelly of social progression.

CHAPTER THREE: THE WOMAN AND GOD

Woman

Woman, as we have come to understand her, was perhaps the first subject men brought under colonial rule: In short, colonialism is a state in which one country extends its reign into another, the inferior country being an extension of the imperialist state (the superior country). Colonized people then become a financial crutch for their colonial masters having their labor power and capital used to strengthen the economy of the imperialists. Note; it is not my claim to say the generally less dominant female position in various societies was born entirely due to male oppression as opposed to aspects of general female nature, and vice versa, however, examining the broad strokes it has become impossible to ignore the similarities between female existence worldwide and a colony under imperial rule: The Africans in the colonies under European rule were purposely given inferior or limited access to education; women worldwide under male rule have had to fight and in some places are still fighting for the right to attend school. The colonies were not allowed to industrialize; women have historically been discouraged from skilled and intellectual fields of work. A colony's labor power and capital is used to strengthen the economy of the imperialist; female labor power has been used to strengthen the male household through various systems such as polygny which among certain peoples like the Igbo or Afghan, an increased number of wives not only became a symbol of power but in practical terms inevitably means increased labor power to a household which ultimately belongs the husband. They may work his fields, mind his children, make the clothes, cook the food and more; in essence they maintain, circulate and increase the wealth of his compound without owning it - just like women in the USA did not have the right to vote until 1920 even though they contributed to the US workforce and economy; in other words women have been used to generate power without being able to possess power just as the low-wage laborer generates capital without being able to possess capital. Going back to polygyny I feel the need to mention I am not against it nor do I think it to be unhealthy under certain circumstances, however, the right of educated choice is where I draw the line between right and wrong. This lack of choice on the part of women in relation to their male counterparts is what makes them oppressed: No woman is entirely feminine nor is any man entirely masculine; the truth is we assume the position of masculine or feminine depending on who we are engaging with at the time. A teacher has assumed a masculine role over a student who assumes a feminine role, the teacher has agreed to lead and the student has agreed to follow; the teacher being masculine does not mean this teacher is male, nor does the student being feminine mean the student is female, but they have assumed the appropriate "gender" among themselves to accomplish a particular goal; the less apt to teach rightly becomes feminine, not female. Women, however, by being denied rights such as the right to be educated or vote, have often been forced into the permanent feminine state of the 'student'; their destiny being out of their control and ripe to be molded by men, who are assumed to be masculine. All people are by default masculine in their want to control their own destiny, but when one is forced into the feminine state of submission by a foreigner imposing their masculinity over them for the fruits of dominion, this form of rape is called imperialism, which is also evident in relations between bourgeois and proletariat. Just as woman has at times been forced into a permanent feminine state, so has the skilled and unskilled proletariat, not only by not owning the means of production but by being, in general, too ill-educated to exceed their position in the business world they belong to. The feminine role will always be second to the masculine, and it is in the feminine state I have chosen to interpret women according to the mind:

In trying to decode the nature of woman it became apparent she is definitely a more inward part of the personality - because across cultures women are a more inward part of society; men usually reserve extroverted roles such as political authority or conquest for themselves. Although due to many a social construct, because the gender of woman's role in society is often feminine - being submissive or complementary to the leading role of men - I have chosen to use the female sex to represent the feminine principle for ease of reading. I was first inclined to compare woman to the emotions, but I realized I had already compared the emotions to wild beasts. Men are as superior to beasts as reason is superior to emotion, yet something superior to emotion yet second to reason is desire just as women are superior to beasts but have often been considered as second to men.

Without the desire for war how does one protect their family in due time, or without sexual desire how does one fulfill marital duties to bring life &

pleasure? But without reason these are fires that burn villages.

Levirate Marriage is a custom which has been practiced in different parts of Africa (such as the Sayyoo Oromoo of Ethiopia, the Nandi of Kenya, and the Shona of Zimbabwe) as well as in the Torah. It is when a widow is given as an entitlement in marriage to the brother of her deceased husband. The unrestraint of desire is the feminine principle; she fills the boundaries of reason, maintaining the house. In societies practicing Levirate marriage a woman dwells either in her father's authority, or her husband's authority, and if the husband die, his brother's authority: they represent the restraint of impulses, allowing them only to act under the authority of reason. Do we not admire the ocean within its confines yet fear the destruction of floods? In the same way the desires must be guided and contained, lest they break forth from their "father's authority" and wreak harlotry within the body, or cross the boundaries of land, flooding the mind with ever changing impulses. Generally speaking, are women not given to impulse - via hormones - more than men by nature? And do not women usually seek men (restraint) they deem greater than themselves be it taller, stronger, richer, a decision maker, wiser, a source of security or more dominant? This is because woman is representative of the inwards from whence comes desire, and so the true measure of a man can many a time be found in the countenance, and well being, and confidence of his wife. According to this logic, the true measure of reason can be found in the extent to which it fulfils healthy desires.

It is nothing newly profound to say masculine and feminine principles exist within both men and women, but the war between them also occurs within us; the war between desire and reason. Although I would not say it is wise to let one's desire rule his house, and it is one's reason, as the head of the 'household', rather than desire, who takes the blame when one acts irresponsibly (through the allegorical lens, an example of this relationship can be found in the Torah; if a man makes a vow his soul is bound by it, but if woman makes a vow under her father or husband's roof and either of them hear it, it is their responsibility to agree and bind her to it, or to make it void so she may be forgiven for not keeping her vow – Numbers 30:1-15), we are often the first to undermine our own desires as being foolish, as trying to lure us away from sound rationale with their persuasiveness; just as men fear their weakness in the presence of women – many schools of thought throughout history from early Church Fathers to indigenous African, Islamic and Hebraic folklore consider women to be a source of contamination of men, as unclean and untrustworthy and ironically at the same time curse the expression of female sexuality by which even the greatest of men have always been conquered, making female sexuality unlike all other things on Earth which men have managed to subdue - we also tend to fear our mental fragility in the face of our truest desires. When we begin to respect our desires as much as we respect our logic - which is not absolute, but a pattern of thought developed in response to life, to be a guide and protector - we will begin to function fluently and freely; our desires not being oppressed by our reasoning and our thoughts not being stifled by our lusts, comparable to Awra Amba, the self-sustaining community in Ethiopia in which men and women work alongside each other equally, effectively and respectfully toward the same goal. Our king, who is reason, has been dethroned and his wives, who are desires, are taken captive by his enemies: Gambling houses and junk food shops heavily target poor areas, these are enemies of our finances and our health, yet our desire for easier opportunities and cheap sustenance are captivated by them. In Islam, the woman is seen as the backbone of the ummah (community), in the Tannakh (psalm 144:12) King David says women will be as cornerstones; desire in man-kind is what holds together the community of his mind, controlling desire you control this community. It is by our misguided desire we keep others in business and ourselves out of pocket, spending on fruitless or harmful pleasures what could instead be used constructively for our benefit. We are constantly chasing the latest 'this' or the most popular 'that' advertized to us by stirring desire, but if our desires were married to and lead by reason, they would not give themselves easily to the sweet words of marketing. The king should consult, but must not be lead by his wives; we should consider, but must not be lead by desire or impulse when we act, for it is our rational mind who will take responsibility for the downfall or prosperity of the kingdom.

"Do nothing without advice; and when thou hast once done, repent not" – Sirach 32:19

God

Gods throughout the ages have been seen as something above man-kind and behind the forces of nature. The invisible hand behind nature is like the invisible science of life man can only speculate and express his partial understanding of. This invisible hand which is absolute, unlike man's understanding, is truth. Truth is above reason, desire, emotion and is timeless. Reason strives for truth taking desire with him, but emotions act responsively rather than speculatively and so have no comprehension of truth although they do respond to it. In the same way a man strives to live like his god, what is it we are aiming for? What among the poorer working class is 'God' but the hope of money they can never make and a lifestyle of pleasurable quick-fixes they can never sustain? Just as the poor, oppressed Christian has always been taught to wait for a fantasy abode in the clouds perceived to be 'Heaven' rather than open his eyes to the destruction of his existing 'Garden of Eden', so the low income proletariat hopes for salvation in the weekend; a fleeting salvation which never truly arrives. One piece of wisdom from the Tannakh for us to consider what is worthy of esteem is this (a similar phrase can also be found in the Qur'an al-Baqarah 2:274):

"Honour the LORD with thy substance, and with the firstfruits of all thine increase" – Proverbs 3:9

But Do You Possess Your Soul?

The principle of this wisdom through the lens of this book makes an interesting meditation and reinforcement to my claim 'God' should be equated with truth. What god (truth) is set at the helm of the mind's kingdom? What do we honor with our substance? If there is no 'god', our reason and desires may come and go and build and destroy and contradict as they please, as a house divided against themselves. If one's reason and desire have no common goal to strive towards they have only to wait to be drawn away and used for the greater good of another, seeing they were idle in their own kingdom. Imagine if we spent our wealth for the cause of 'God'; a higher truth we are striving for. On how much foolish conversation, fruitless investment or pleasure-seeking could we waste our substance of time, finance or knowledge if we spent our wealth for an absolute greater good? Knowing your 'God' has all to do with knowing yourself. It is up to each man to place something above his own ego lest he be ruled by his ego, as it is the nature of man to place himself, or his truth, above the head of those who have no god, or at least no god he respects. We said earlier to ask "who am I" is to ask "what is my occupation", now we see asking "Who is my God?" is to ask "What do I honor in the spending of my substance?"... Do we spend ourselves on sustainability & functionality? Do we even have substance to spend?

As the decision maker, or reason of a society, all must serve the King. But the King must be accountable to one higher truth than himself, for without this, only a self serving tyranny remains. Knowing God is above man and truth is above his reason, also knowing truth should saturate right reason just as God should dwell in the hearts of righteous men, one should always consider which god – be it vanity, opulence, or love - has saturated him with its laws, and which truth he wishes to serve.

The Babylonian god Marduk, son of Ea, is also argued to be a deified version of the biblical Nimrod, son of Kush, who was a mighty imperialistic "hunter" and builder of civilization, according to the Hebrews, who endured Babylonian captivity, an oppressor. In the creation myth associated with Marduk, he became the head god – note, in Hebraic thought the term 'god' can also be synonymous with a human ruler or form of government - by defeating Tiamat, who was the most feared in a war amongst the gods. After defeating her, Marduk said this:

"Blood I will mass and cause bones to be. I will establish a savage, 'man' shall be his name. Verily savage-man I will create. He shall be charged with the service of the gods that they might be at ease"

Marduk, Nimrod, the imperialist, has said he will create man as a savage for the service of the 'gods': in the chapter "Wild Beasts and the Land" we explored how the working man and woman are kept in a state of ignorance and emotionalism, living as beasts. In the chapter "The King and the Military" it was said we are kept in a state of distraction by mediums such as Television and music. Let us weigh this analysis against what was described by the infamous communist writer Karl Marx:

"From what has been said, it is manifest, that, in a free nation, where slaves are not allowed of, the surest wealth consists in a multitude of laborious poor; for besides, that they are the never-failing nursery of fleets and armies, without them there could be no enjoyment, and no product of any country could be valuable."

In other words, these are those 'charged with the service of the gods'. Marx goes on to say:

"To make the society happy and people easier

under the meanest circumstances, it is requisite that great numbers of them should be ignorant as well as poor; knowledge both enlarges and multiplies our desires, and the fewer things a man wishes for, the more easily his necessities may be supplied"

Ignorance and poverty is the state of the savage-man. It is in the spending of our substance, in thought, in the giving of our labor power, in perpetual servitude of capital, in perpetual worship of Marduk, one who has not considered this reality and strove to live above the nature of the beast, becomes the savage rather than being merely ill-educated; a slave rather than merely a prisoner of war.

CHAPTER FOUR: NEO-COLONIALISM AND BELIEF

Neo-colonialism

Dissatisfaction keeps a flame gnawing at the wick, and contentedness is a polite form of death.

Neo-colonialism is a state in which the colonized country is nominally free, but is colonized from the outside and dictated to in more subtle ways like unfair trade relations. When Haiti, which was France's most profitable colony, declared independence from France in 1804 after revolting and defeating Napoleon's armies, France demanded compensation due to their loss of slave labor (Haitians) and would not recognize Haiti as independent unless they paid. The debt was today's equivalent of roughly 15 billion US dollars, which was demanded of a population of roughly half a million people. France cut off all trade with Haiti, stationing battleships around its shores threatening invasion and re-enslavement of the Haitian people. Haiti, being a small population of freed slaves, had no choice but to pay, and did not finish paying off this debt until 1947, 140 years after the "abolition" of the slave trade! Just consider for a moment how this alone would affect Haiti's development as a country, then consider why debt has become a normal part of life for the working class, even down to 'innocent' bank overdrafts and credit cards. The truth is, most people cannot sustain themselves let alone advance themselves on their own wages. Fountain Hughes (1848-1957), a former slave who had his experiences voice recorded, boasted in the fact he did not owe anyone a dime and encouraged others to only buy what they can pay for. Why would a former slave have such disdain for debt? And why is the working class so blind to its binding role in their own enslavement? It is because the working class have some mobility outside the plantation and thus the illusion of freedom. Rome held a more subtle form of neo-colonialism in the minds of its own foreign citizens; unlike other hostile nations it allowed its people freedom to worship their own gods within its walls, but ultimately homage had to be paid to the Emperor and he would still have financial and political sway over the people - considering in ancient times religion and politics were intertwined, this meant they belonged to their religion in name only, but in reality they were still just as much the property of Rome. To give people the illusion of religious freedom means a greater influx of citizens who can pay taxes and build the state. This nominal freedom creates contentedness which hushes the human desire of progression; this is also why slave owners in the USA allowed slaves small liberties like dressing up on Sundays if it made them merrier workers. Yet in all this 'freedom', what happens when the laws of one's religion contradicts the culture of Rome, as in the case of the Jews? What if the wage laboring class is no longer content with higher pay, which may just as easily be counterbalanced by higher costs of living, and want a more complete independence? It is only then we see how truly free someone is. It is the same form of neo-colonialism suggesting to people they are doing well because they have nice assets, but in reality they are slaving away to pay off tuition fees, interest on loans and other traps marketed as avenues to success (which technically means they do not own the value of their assets because they are in debts often times greater than what they appear to own). The lower working class are put in debt just to pay for rent, to travel, feed their children and any other thing a normal adult would need to live a normal life. The children are kept in this cycle of "fending for themselves" by borrowing from their oppressors, living stacked on top of one another, unable to sustain themselves on their own earnings, yet being encouraged to dream big and follow their dreams, which, to the uneducated, often means "blindly chase what you think you are good at and get upset when they don't buy your mix-tape". This "follow your dreams" deception is the same lie fed to the African colonies, this lie in economic terms is what is called "comparative advantage"; comparative advantage basically means it is better for a country to pursue what it is good at producing rather than learning new skills or technologically advancing itself in anything new in order to change its economic set up. For example, this would mean because one country is good at growing corn it should specify in growing corn and it will eventually find wealth through this, but not mentioned to the corn growing country is the other country manufacturing cars: The former will never earn as much as the latter in dreams or real life and so will always be below in the food chain, the purely agricultural country below the industrialized country. The country is told to keep from learning new skills, when this learning of new skills by studying others, or "emulation", is what enables nations to innovate beyond easily achievable unskilled basics and develop themselves, giving them more to bargain with in the world market which is increasingly fond of new technologies. In the same way low wage earners are fed this mentality of applying for jobs they think they are suited to so they will find happiness, as though practical skills like plumbing or electrical engineering aren't possible to be learned by everyone. By this mentality we do not go where the money or necessity is, but we follow what we think we are good at even into an unprofitable grave, just like the colonies our unwillingness to forget the fairytales of comparative advantage and learn new skills is part of what hinders us economically. Just as a country must industrialize to become competitively independent, the individual must be able to manufacture some product of necessity in order to be at least self-employed – and self employment is only the second stage in possible financial evolution (from employee to self employed to business owner to investor). One example of the delusions of comparative advantage is the mentality of many young males in the cities; many want to be rich and famous, they try to emulate the products they see marketed to them rather than emulating the templates of good business. For this reason you will find no shortage of young men who say "I want to do rap music" and "I'm making my own clothing line", going head first into highly competitive industries in hopes of succeeding like every other person doing the exact same thing even though nobody really needs the average rapper and the city is certainly not in need of clothes. Of those who say "I want to do music" you will not find so many who are willing to learn how to tune a piano let alone learn to program a music software or even study the music business. Of those who say "I'm making my own clothing line" you will hardly find one who is willing to learn to sew let alone tailor their own clothes or study the history of clothing's societal impact or importance. We are so prideful as not to respect the arts, and we are such sheep in the way of progression, following wolves in hopes of salvation. Branding strategist

Terri Trespicio said the notion of following your passion is an "elitist" concept, as passion is a feeling susceptible to change and therefore not a good measurement to judge by. Passion is not a good measurement because reason is thrown out of the window! Again we see how the thought process of the people is encouraged to dwell in the beast state of emotion. Passion at best could be desire, but without reason following passion is a vain pursuit. The reason for this misleading 'elitist' advice is because the almost hedonistic life of the ruling class is a suit which can only fit 1% of the population, therefore blinders are put on the imagination of the workers; they are taught to strive to become the 1%, to strive to become landlords in the same manner, to strive to conduct business in the same manner, to squeeze themselves as the 99% into the suit of the 1%, which is the unattainable Nirvana for those in the land of the wretched, rather than to think outside the rules of their current reality, making them incapable of changing it.

There is a West African saying "No one gives a pig to a hyena to keep", yet we leave our lives and the lives of our children in the hands of a system which does not care about us beyond the profit it can accumulate from us; from landlords to business owners and all manner of debt traps observable, the unskilled labor force is being slowly replaced by machinery along with the skilled laborers who do not make themselves irreplaceable by individuality and mastery; cashiers are replaced by self service machines, musicians by music software, there are even machines capable of brick-laying and 3D printers capable of creating houses, therefore it is beyond foolish to rely solely on wage labor which can be replaced by technology, especially at minimum wage. First those in the factories and plantations of the 'Third World' will be crushed, and they are being crushed, by all the ills of being disposable and replaceable unskilled workers which leaves them helplessly subject to their neocolonial masters, but this can only work its way up, and it is working its way up to the lower class in the developed world, which is evident in the widening wealth gap - the more the capitalist finds cheaper sources of labor, the more the worker, who is dependent upon him, becomes disposable, and as we see from around the 1500's, there is nothing new under the sun;

"To keep international market prices high, spice production was deliberately limited. Almost the entire population of the Banda Islands, the source of nutmeg, was killed and replaced with European employees and slave labor in the fields" – Sally Blundell, journalist.

If 'God' is the aim of human evolution, why should man remain reliant on work as a hand-me-down from someone else, knowing an attribute of God is self-sufficiency?

Belief

If land is time, beast is emotion, woman is desire, king is reason and God is truth then I would interpret the inward economic state as one's belief system - consider what was said earlier to ask "Who is my God?" is to ask "What do I honor in the spending of my substance?"; that 'substance', in this case, is thought, which finances our words and actions just as the king's economy finances his military. The belief system is also a commercial one, and there is a market place among people in the mind; where the strength of individual currency is backed by their integrity and reputation – there is an Igbo saying "to have people is better than to have money". This market-place has been in ruin since we stopped thinking for ourselves concerning our socio-economic situation; that is to say we stopped manufacturing and became consumers being sold an entire destiny by foreign kings, at the expense of not only independent produce but independent thought. Even under a nominal freedom of thought how many of us can truly be ourselves? It is our responsibility to study in order to regain control of our figurative environment, livestock, nation, economy and our truth. To achieve this is to take the crown of your life from your enemies and place it where it belongs; upon your own head. Consider this.

CHAPTER FIVE: THE GLORY OF KINGS

The Glory of Kings

"and those Negroes make the best servants, that have been slaves in their own country, for they that have been kings and great men there are generally lazy, haughty, and obstinate"

Among American slave-owners those who had been kings in their own country were noted to have made the worst slaves due to a lofty attitude, and Frederick Douglas said Education makes a man unfit to be a slave; that is to say what one is willing to remain subject to is heavily dependent upon how one sees himself in his own mind, and how one sees himself is heavily dependent upon his indoctrination – people would not be slaves to a base intellect and nature; gangsters in the slums of Jamaica would not be persuaded to kill each other over political affiliation, women in parts of Africa would not allow their daughters to be circumcised, people would not allow themselves to dwell in low self-esteem, and the oppressed worldwide would not accept their condition as the will of God if only they were educated to believe they were worth more; more than the beast egotistical man does not respect. A king must be well groomed before he is given power, and so we must consider the state of the mind before we contemplate gaining power ourselves. The place and time to gather the military of the mind is often in pit of "lowly estate" or poverty – Marcus Garvey learned self-sufficiency when left in a pit by his father, Malcolm Little became Malcolm X when in jail and Gandhi became sensitive to his own tyranny when in war. Although the life of the King is largely one of control over external affairs, with freedom concerning finance and time, the life of a good king is also one of self control, with discipline concerning productivity and pleasure, for which finance and time are sacrificed. How can one control their entire destiny when they cannot control themselves? As the entire universe expands, so do our habits, and the consequences thereof.

In meditation I have transcended the pit, and I have concluded this: Stagnant water is unhealthy, but in the ebb and flow of poverty and wealth, of sacrifice and reward, of investment and increase, there are some who are not tyrants only because they are poor, and some who are not humble only because they are rich; these are morally swayed by circumstance, unlike truth, which is immovable in the currents of external affairs. Though we must be prudent in order to secure a future for ourselves and our children, the cycles of life happen to us all, but it is our immovability in our desire to do right - as far as we can understand what is right - which proves us to be heroes or mercenaries. Therefore the glory of kings, or the glory of one who possess their own soul, is not material but moral, and so by virtue a king is a king in poverty or riches just as Marcus Garvey said a strong man is strong anywhere, and now I will end:

The glory of kings is not in the multitude of his soldiers, nor is the greatness of one's self in the multitude of words, but it is in the justice upheld by the military and truth in one's speech:

- "What is the beauty of a man?" Al'Abbas asked the Prophet [Mohammed, pbuh]. "It is in his language", he replied.

- "As when one sifteth with a sieve, the refuse remaineth; so the filth of man in his talk" – Sirach 27:4

The glory of kings is not in the splendor of worldly possessions, nor is the greatness of one's self in their opulence, but it is in a righteous manner of acquisition and generosity:

- "Woe unto him that buildeth his house without righteousness, and his chambers by wrong; that useth his neighbour's service without wages, and giveth him not for his work" – Jeremiah 22:13
- "The generous person is nearer to God and the people, and is nearer to paradise and further from hell; the miser is far from God and the people, and a long way from paradise, but nearer to hell." – Islamic proverb

The glory of kings is not in the extent in rule over cities and towns, nor is the greatness of one's self in the reach of one's influence, but it is in the administration of justice and how functionally one governs their life:

- "When the righteous are in authority, the people rejoice; but when the wicked

beareth rule, the people mourn" – Proverbs 29:2
- The just ruler awards justice and does not perpetrate injustice and wickedness. For, the unjust ruler is ill-starred and will not last, because the Prophet stated that, "sovereignty endures even when there is unbelief, but will not endure when there is injustice." – Amr b. al-'As

Dear kings:

"The best amongst people is the one who is most beneficial to people" - Al-Tabarani.

"The greatest among you shall be your servant"- Matthew 23:11

Until all are captives of equitable reason, freedom and war will always co-exist.

CHAPTER SIX

Chapter six is up to you.

But Do You Possess Your Soul?

HIDDEN CHAPTER: FREEDOM AND WAR

These are some of my passing thoughts on freedom and war, which may be revised at a later time. They may be useful or at least a delightful muse, so I have decided to include them merely as extra reading:

Due to a brutal history we assume colonization – the expansion of a political power into another's territory – to be immoral and wrong. Colonizers usually believe they possess some God-given quality granting them the right to rule for the sake of the world, and those poor savages who would be so lost without them. To shun this attitude would be hypocritical considering human nature; no matter how we protest the expansionist in his efforts to secure already occupied territories, we ourselves are active practitioners of intellectual colonization. By our words we seek to spread the dominion of our ideals, we declare war on inferior thinking for the sake of our god (our greater good) and settle our logic in the hearts of men. The evolution of thought, as opposed to remaining in ignorance, is predicated upon violence, as we too, after destroying old ideas, seek to defend our territory from infiltration we deem contrary to our existence as a state. We war not against flesh and blood, because we, in the realm of flesh and blood, cannot kill an idea, but we can propagandize and attack the lifestyle of others. Flesh succumbs to the sword, but true death comes by the thought: the idea, being un-killable by hand, and able to penetrate the heart regardless of flesh, is man's most powerful form of military, and so for this reason the pen is mightier than the sword. Considering this, a people who interpret and write their own history and a person who interprets and defines their own identity, telling their own story, both have demonstrated a great power, which until very recently, most Africans, Indigenous Americans and Australians as well as women worldwide could not enjoy.

War is not wrong, war is the result of resistance to wrong. All wickedness is unsustainable, therefore by 'wrong' I mean that which is unsustainable, for it is often by sustainability man measures right and wrong: It is wrong to indulge in drugs because although it may be pleasurable, the body cannot sustain this activity over time. It is wrong to betray trust because although you may have some selfish benefit, broken trust cannot sustain a friendship. It is wrong to steal because although one may gain, an entire society of thieves cannot sustain a functional economy; saying this, if one were to create an equilibrium between a class of thieves and a class of victims, this may be sustainable as long as the latter are kept oblivious to being cheated – according to the Chinese war strategist Sun Tzu, all warfare is based on deception, making this also an act of war, one against the people. The class of thieves, who one may assume to be the bourgeois, may also be our 'leaders' who have established a monopoly over socio-political thought, yet have failed elevate the standard of thought amongst the people, which is observable through the ineffective ideals and superstitions of the age. Just as the oppressed have always had to fight in one way or another, – even in peaceful protest; the bus boycott of Martin Luther King Jr. did violence to bus company finance – the indoctrinated must study in order to correct and reclaim themselves. Freedom, and freedom of thought is a beautiful human struggle, but freedom, and freedom of thought are also a prelude to further violence where one is oppressed by way of another's freedom.

Freedom, due to the timeless human desire for it, is often assumed to be right and just. But how about intellectual freedom? Moral freedom? Is it not by freedom we exploit the weak? In fact, by freedom man often brings himself into further bondage; by unrestrained, riotous living one becomes a slave to addiction and debt. Freedom of thought means freedom of action, and freedom of action means disunity amongst people who differ in thought, although they, being social creatures, need each other to survive. Therefore to bring the less civilized under colonial rule and the less intelligent under dominion may be seen as a preventative measure against anarchy. Maybe it is not wrong of superiors to convince their subjects life is only worth living in the context created for them - because by the systems our governments create our worlds are held in place - but maybe the subject, being unhappy in this context, is also wrong to take their word for it without rebellion, seeing they had survived before the intrusive arrogance of their colonizers. Even in love freedom does not exist, compromise and surrender allow us to live with each other. Freedom is an illusion, freedom is free from color, free from taste, free from restraint, free from law, free from context; freedom is no existence at all, even for those in charge. Because of this I conclude freedom, deep down, is not what men are fighting for, nor should it be what we fight for, but what we desire is a respectable, sustainable context to dwell within. For this reason salvation is not in freedom, but in bondage to the right masters. The external struggle for freedom and individuality must simultaneously be fought alongside the internal struggle to bear the yoke of responsibility to our neighbor, until the war-ridden evolution of human interaction has been satisfied to the point of harmony. This harmony, bound by law, is the salvation called "freedom" we have sought since the beginning of inequity.

But Do You Possess Your Soul?

Quoted sources in chronological order:

M.F.Brooks, 1995, *A modern Translation of the KEBRA NAGAST (The Glory of Kings)*, The Red Sea Press, Inc.

T.Weisz, 2006, *THE KAIFENG STONE INSCRIPTIONS: the Legacy of the Jewish Community in Ancient China*, iUniverse

W.Rodney, 2012, *How Europe Underdeveloped Africa*, Pambazuka Press, Cape Town, Dakar, Nairobi and Oxford

Pilger, John. "John Pilger –The Secret Country – The First Australians.pt1/4." Online video clip. Commonagenet. YouTube, 24 Jan. 2012. Web. 27 Jul. 2016.

T.Parfitt, 2013, *Black Jews in Africa and the Americas,* Harvard University Press, Cambridge, Massachusetts / London, England

Trespicio, Terri. "Stop searching for your passion | Terri Trespicio | TEDxKC." Online video clip. TEDx Talks. Youtube, 14 Sep. 2015. Web. 27 Jul. 2016.

K.Marx, 2011, *Capital: Volume one: A Critique of Political Economy*, Dover Publications Inc.

I.Khaldun, Danyal Nicholson, 2013, *THE MUQADDIMAH: An Introduction to History*, The Olive Press

M.Mullin, 1976, *American Negro Slavery: A DOCUMENTARY HISTORY*, University of South Carolina Press

Dr.M.A.J.Beg, 2007, *Wisdom of Islamic Civilization – Miscellany of Islamic Quotations*, Dr.M.A.J.Beg, Cambridge

The KJV Bible, the apocrypha & the Qur'an were also used to form this work.

ABOUT THE AUTHOR

Poet, philosopher and visual artist Aaron Lawrence, who also uses the name Ezra Aharon - Ezra, in Hebrew means to be a help or an aid – is a creative with a vision to inspire dialogue and thought among people concerning realities of human existence. Believing self-education, in more ways than one, is the seed of progression, he aims to re-acquaint more of society with the practicalities of reading and self-analysis.

Made in the USA
Charleston, SC
28 September 2016